# Just as you are

Suzy Senior • illustrated by Estelle Corke

'Where are you off to, Donkey?' asked Squirrel.

'I'm just having a plod around,' replied Donkey, with a flick of his long, fluffy ears. 'I'm going to talk with the God of all Things.'

Squirrel gasped.
'The God of all Things?
Really – just as you are?
Aren't you a bit...
scruffy, Donkey?'

'Oh!' said Donkey.
He hadn't thought about
that. Donkeys were
strong and hairy and
they worked hard.
As far as he knew,
they always looked
scruffy!

'Here, wear this!' suggested Squirrel. She pulled a bedsheet off the washing line, and spread it over Donkey's back. It covered his sticking-out fur.

'Much better!' announced Squirrel, cheerily. 'Off you go.'

Donkey set off down the lane. Soon, he saw Cat, sunbathing.

'Hey, slow down! Where are you going, Donkey?' asked Cat.

'Just for a little walk.' Donkey grinned. 'I'm going to talk with the God of all Things.'

'The God of all Things? Excellent!' Cat looked impressed. 'But are you going just as you are? What about your ears – they're kind of funny and fuzzy! Maybe you could you wear a hat or something?'

Donkey wasn't sure. He was already wearing a bedsheet, and that was very itchy.

'Here, try this bucket,' said Cat, helpfully. 'It will cover your ears up nicely.'

Donkey put the bucket on his head. It didn't fit very well, but he could just about see out.

'Purrfect!' said Cat. 'See you soon.'

Donkey carried on...
until he nearly stepped on Mouse.

'Hey!' squeaked Mouse.
'Watch where you're going!'

'Sorry!' cried Donkey, jumping back.
'The bucket fell down over my eyes!
I'm going to talk with the God of all Things,'
he explained.

'What?' huffed Mouse. 'Just as you are?'
His forehead wrinkled.

'Are you sure you've been good enough? You just nearly squashed a mouse... and yesterday you ate the farmer's flowers.'

'Oh dear!' sighed Donkey, sadly. 'They just looked so yummy. I didn't know they belonged to anyone.' He felt terrible. Maybe Mouse was right! He tried not to cry. 'Goodbye Mouse,' he sniffed.

Sadly, Donkey wandered towards the river. How could he possibly talk to the God of all Things now?

He leaned on the fence and
scratched his chin.

Suddenly, CRACK! The fence tipped over. Donkey's legs waved in the air as he tumbled right down the bank and into the river! SPLASH! The sheet floated off, and the slimy green weeds tangled in his tail. The bucket rolled after him, filling up with water and some very surprised fish!

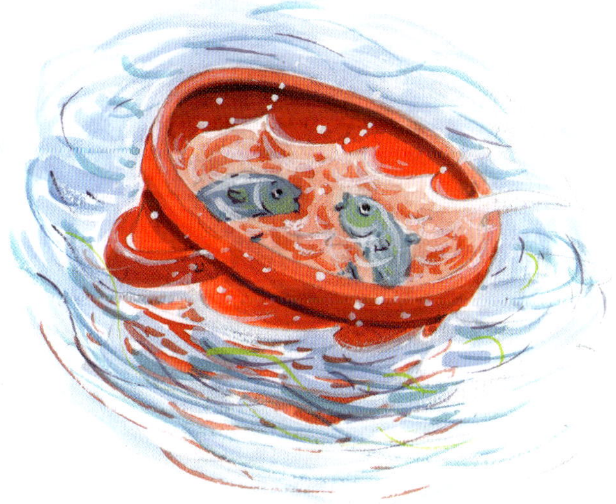

Donkey struggled over the slippery stones, until finally he got back on his feet. He flopped onto the bank. He looked terrible!

'Oh God of all Things,' he whispered, 'how can I talk to you now? I'm scruffy and soaked and sad and muddy and naughty. I even have funny-shaped ears and green stuff in my tail!'

He sat in silence
for a moment.
Then he realised.
He HAD just
talked to the
God of all
Things. It felt
good – and
he somehow
felt certain
that the God of
all Things was
listening!

So, he carried on –
all afternoon – some
of the time talking,

and some of the time just
sitting happily with The God
of All Things.

When the sun started to set, Donkey gathered up the bucket and the bedsheet and went home. Back at the farm, the other animals were sitting together on the wall. Squirrel's mouth dropped open.

'Whatever happened to you?' she cried. 'You look scruffier than ever!'

'Yes, I do,' agreed Donkey. 'I AM quite scruffy and hairy. I've got huge ears, and sometimes I make mistakes. BUT, the God of all Things made me just as I am,' he said simply, 'and he loves me just as I am!'

He grinned at Mouse,
Squirrel and Cat.
'And...' he said,

'...he loves
YOU too,
just as
YOU are!'

PALM TREE

Buxhall, Stowmarket, Suffolk IP14 3BW. Tel: +44 (0) 1449 737978
E-mail: info@kevinmayhew.com www.kevinmayhew.com

Product Code: 1600016 ISBN: 978 1 83858 073 5


Publishing Director: Annette Reynolds
Art Director: Gerald Rogers
Pre-production: Doug Hewitt


Printed and bound in China